CLASSIC WISDOM COLLECTION

TODAY'S QUESTIONS. TIMELESS ANSWERS.

Looking for time-tested guidance for the dilemmas of the spiritual life? Find it in the company of the wise spiritual masters of our Catholic tradition.

Comfort in Hardship: Wisdom from Thérèse of Lisieux

Inner Peace: Wisdom from Jean-Pierre de Caussade

Life's Purpose: Wisdom from John Henry Newman

Path of Holiness: Wisdom from Catherine of Siena

Secrets of the Spirit: Wisdom from Luis Martinez

A Simple Life: Wisdom from Jane Frances de Chantal

Solace in Suffering: Wisdom from Thomas à Kempis

Strength in Darkness: Wisdom from John of the Cross

Forthcoming volumes will include wisdom from:
Francis de Sales
James Alberione

D0937547

Comfort in Hardship

CLASSIC WISDOM COLLECTION

Comfort in Hardship

Wisdom from Thérèse of Lisieux

Foreword and compiled by Germana Santos, FSP

Pauline
BOOKS & MEDIA
Boston

Library of Congress Cataloging-in-Publication Data

Thérèse, de Lisieux, Saint, 1873-1897.
  [Selections. English. 2011]
  Comfort in hardship : wisdom from Thérèse of Lisieux / foreword and compiled by Germana Santos.
     p. cm. -- (Classic wisdom collection)
  Includes bibliographical references (p. 69).
  ISBN 0-8198-1588-8 (pbk.)
  1. Spirituality--Catholic Church. I. Santos, Germana. II. Title. III. Series.
  BX2179.T49E5 2011
  282.092--dc22

                                2010038174

Published by Pauline Books & Media, 50 Saint Pauls Avenue, Boston, MA 02130-3491.

www.pauline.org.

Printed in the U.S.A.

Pauline Books & Media is the publishing house of the Daughters of St. Paul, an international congregation of women religious serving the Church with the communications media.

1 2 3 4 5 6 7 8 9   15 14 13 12 11

Contents

X

Source of Strength

Notes

Bibliography

Foreword

Gray clouds hung over Lisieux that late December day as I arrived in the city with another Daughter of Saint Paul. Despite the icy gusts of wind, we stopped to look up a small hill and admire the magnificent Basilica dedicated to Saint Thérèse of the Child Jesus. We were finally in this industrial city in Normandy, renowned for the attractive French saint whose life and writings have captured the Catholic imagination. Thérèse Martin lived most of her life there, so today her name is synonymous with her city: Saint Thérèse of Lisieux.

I had wanted to visit France since I began to study the French language at the age of ten. The textbook pictures had filled my young mind with delightful visions of a land full of charm and appeal. Many years later, during graduate studies in Rome, Italy, I had the opportunity to travel to the land of my dreams. And the visit did not disappoint. I visited some sites connected with notable French saints such as Bernadette Soubirous, Catherine Labouré, Francis de Sales, Jane Frances de Chantal, John Vianney, and more. But the city of Lisieux, the home of Thérèse, enchanted me and left a deep impression. I was walking in her footsteps, looking at many of the buildings that she saw, and breathing the air of her hometown.

Wrapped in our winter jackets, gloves, and scarves to protect us from the blustery cold, we walked to sites of major interest: the Basilica of Saint Thérèse where her parents are buried, the Carmel of Lisieux where Thérèse lived her hidden life of prayer and virtue, and the parish church of Saint Peter where her family worshiped. But for me the highlight was Les Buissonnets—the Martins' lovely home, which Thérèse always loved.

Thérèse was born in Alençon on January 2, 1873, the last child of Louis Martin and Zélie-Marie Guérin Martin. Louis was a watchmaker and jeweler, and Zélie learned the delicate art of lace-making. They had a happy marriage and were deeply religious. In fact, this holy couple was beatified in 2008. Of their nine children, four died in infancy. The five others were all girls. Marie, Pauline, Céline, and Thérèse entered Carmel, and Léonie became a Visitation nun. Zélie, a vivacious woman, was a tender and patient mother, and Louis was a devoted and doting father. The Martin home vibrated with laughter, goodness, faith, prayer, respect, and intense affection among all its members. The depth of Zélie's faith spilled out into her everyday life through her daily attendance at Mass, and also in her work and home life. Marie, the oldest daughter, writing to Pauline, the second daughter who was away at school, presented a lively picture of their mother: "It is really something to arrange a May-altar in this house; Mama is too difficult, more difficult than the Blessed Virgin! It has to have hawthorn branches reaching up to the ceiling, walls covered in greens, etc., etc. . . ."[1]

But suffering soon knocked on the family's door. Zélie died of breast cancer at the age of forty-five, when Thérèse was only four years old. Brokenhearted, Louis Martin moved the family to the town of Lisieux in order to be closer to Zélie's surviving brother, Isidore Guérin, a pharmacist. He and his wife, Céline, had two daughters.

The sincere faith that marked Louis Martin and his five daughters permitted them to live a joyful, serene life in the beautiful two-story brick home that was Les Buissonnets. The Martins were financially well off and lacked nothing. Writing many years later, Marie referred to Thérèse (and by inclusion, all of the Martins) as "having lived in opulence in her childhood."[2] Even today, I recall my impression of the understated wealth I observed when visiting their lovely home. The oak round table in the dining room is surrounded by dark wooden chairs, with seats and back cushions covered in brocade. On the second floor, a glass case displays various items that belonged to Thérèse, including some toys, a dress, and jewelry. A gold cross and chain stand out, shining as brightly as they must have when Thérèse wore them over her beautiful clothes, with her blonde hair falling in soft curls.

Thérèse was treated lovingly and with great tenderness, and was shown many external signs of affection by her father and her sisters. Thérèse knew that they loved her, and she basked in the attention of her entire family. She trusted them implicitly. In turn she directed her trust to God, offered her tender love to Christ, and developed a warm devotion for the Virgin Mary.

Drawn to God from her childhood, Thérèse felt the desire to enter Carmel at the age of fifteen. Although she was denied permission to do so by the local religious authorities because she was too young, she took advantage of a pilgrimage to Rome to pose her request to Pope Leo XIII. He told her to abide by the decision of the superiors, and that she would enter if it was God's will.

Eventually, her trust and persistence were rewarded, and she entered Carmel. Her efforts at living the hidden virtues, with much love and abandonment in God, led to a unique type of spirituality that she called "her little way," one that would catch fire throughout the Church.

The "little way" was indeed one of Therese's greatest contributions to a world hungering for love. "I am only a child, powerless and weak, and yet it is my weakness that gives me the boldness of offering myself as *VICTIM of Your Love, O Jesus!*"[3]

For nine years, Thérèse lived a hidden, quiet life in Carmel, intensely faithful to her call to holiness. However, her life was all too brief. She died on September 30, 1897, at the age of twenty-four, consumed by illness and racked by extreme pain. She was finally delivered from the sufferings of this earth and raised into the arms of the God she loved without measure. Pope Pius XI canonized her on May 17, 1925, and Pope John Paul II declared her a doctor of the Church on October 19, 1997.

This book, part of the *Classic Wisdom Collection*, is drawn from the writings of Thérèse and from her family's correspondence. It centers on the theme: *"One family's journey of separation, illness, and death."* The reference is to the family of Thérèse herself. Life smiled kindly on the Martin family due to the love among the parents and the children, their deep faith, and their financial stability and good fortune. But *separation, illness, and death* do not discriminate.

As already mentioned, cancer robbed Thérèse of her mother. Later, but while still a child, Thérèse suffered a mysterious illness that still puzzles experts today—was it a psychological disorder? A physical one? We don't know. Her sisters entered the convent and "left" her—separations that were a considerable hardship for her sensitive nature. At the end of his life, Thérèse's father exhibited strange and frightening behavior. The mild, gentle, affectionate man who wouldn't "hurt a cat," one day was found wielding his gun and babbling about war and invasions. After being disarmed, he was taken to what was then called "a mental hospital," where he remained for three years. The evidence available to us today is insufficient to determine the exact nature of his illness (could it have been a type of dementia?), but the ordeal caused unbearable suffering for Thérèse and her sisters.

And then Thérèse suffered her final illness, the tuberculosis that ravaged her body and tested her spirit so that she lived a time of excruciating pain and spiritual darkness.

How did her family cope with so many hardships? How did Thérèse herself endure the various afflictions in her family and religious community, besides her own physical and mental pain? In this book, we listen to her voice recounting some of the most painful events in her family's history. She also offers her stance on human suffering, and reveals her intimate relationship with Christ, which provided the meaning and strength she needed to carry on. Thérèse walks us into a world of deep love and intense suffering. She helps us move beyond self-pity or anger. She shows us that suffering, whether emotional or physical, is no cause for surprise or shame, and love makes it easier to bear.

In her letters and her autobiographical narrative, Thérèse shows extraordinary love of God. In itself, her life was sheltered, provincial, and ordinary. But her love for God was wide, passionate, profoundly faithful, and extraordinary! We can find inspiration in Thérèse's uncommon devotion and dedication, and her immeasurable capacity for loving God through Christ. Because of her limitless trust, she knew that no suffering goes unrewarded or wasted. We, too, should desire to accept our sufferings peacefully, placing ourselves trustingly in God's good hands. His Son, Jesus Christ, who experienced the violence of human torment, understands our own pain. In all things, we only need to remain childlike in our confidence in God's loving goodness. As Thérèse wrote: "It is confidence and nothing but confidence that must lead us to Love. . . ."⁴ And: "I understand so well that it is only love that can make us pleasing to God, that this love is the only good that I ambition. Jesus is pleased to show me the only road which leads to this divine furnace, and this road is the *abandonment* of the little child who sleeps without fear in her Father's arms. . . ."⁵

Following the spiritual propensity of her times, and through the use of mystical language, Thérèse expresses her love not only by accepting her suffering, but even by seeking it. "My God, I accept everything out of love for you: if you will it, I really want to suffer even to the point of dying of grief. Jesus was content with this acceptance."⁶ Our modern sensibilities recoil at the concept of asking for suffering. But Thérèse's motivation was always to show her love for Christ, since her whole life had become a hymn of love. She was at the heights of the spiritual life, the point where the person is so transformed in God that the thought of suffering no longer disturbs it. The little practices of virtue, or any difficulties, the small "pinpricks," as she called them, or the big crosses—all were occasions to participate in Jesus Christ's passion and death and to show her love. After all, didn't Jesus himself say, "No one has greater love than this, to lay down one's life for one's friends" (Jn 15:13)?

Thérèse's style of writing calls for a word of explanation, especially for those who are new to it. Her memoirs may not appeal to everyone. Even some Teresian scholars have been initially put off by her flowery prose, full of endearing diminutives, superlatives, and exclamations. One of her biographers called it "the usual conventions of elevated discourse." [7] But in comparing her work with those of her contemporaries, we discover that she reflects the style of her times and the religious piety then common in France. A closer reading of Thérèse's writings, however, reveals very insightful concepts about God, the spiritual life, and human nature. Below the surface of her elaborate style, we find a profound doctrine of Christian discipleship that is demanding and attainable only to those who cultivate deep faith and a familiar relationship with God.

The following chapters contain material drawn from letters and other writings of Thérèse. Explanatory material is set off in italics. Now, with Saint Thérèse as guide, we can explore the spiritual secrets that gave her the strength to face every difficulty, loss, and suffering with serenity and trust. May her teaching help us to do the same.

I

Story of a Soul

One winter evening in the Carmel of Lisieux, Thérèse was recounting stories of her childhood to her sisters, Sister Marie of the Sacred Heart (Marie) and Mother Agnes of Jesus (Pauline). Fascinated, Marie suggested that Pauline, then prioress, ask Thérèse to write down her memories. This is how Thérèse's autobiographical writings came about. Here Thérèse is introducing the work; the letters from her family reveal the love that surrounded her.

Springtime story of a little white flower written by herself and dedicated to the Reverend Mother Agnes of Jesus.

It is to you, dear Mother, to you who are doubly my Mother,[1] that I come to confide the story of my soul. . . . I'm going to be doing only one thing: I shall begin to sing what I must sing eternally: *"The Mercies of the LORD"* (Ps 88:2).

Before taking up my pen, I knelt before the statue of Mary (the one that has given so many proofs of the maternal preferences of heaven's Queen for our family), and I begged her to guide my hand that it trace no line displeasing to her.[2]

It is not, then, my life, properly so-called, that I am going to write; it is my *thoughts* on the graces God deigned to grant me. I find myself at a period in my life when I can cast a glance on the past; my soul has matured in the crucible of exterior and interior trials. And now, like a flower strengthened by the storm, I can raise my head and see the words of Psalm 22[3] realized in me: "The LORD is my Shepherd, I shall not want; he makes me lie down in green pastures. He leads me beside still waters; he restores my soul. Even though I walk through the valley of the shadow of death, I fear no evil; for you are with me . . ." [Ps 22:1–4]. To me the Lord has always been "merciful and good, slow to anger and abounding in steadfast love" (Ps 102:8).[4]

In the story of my soul, up until my entrance into Carmel, I distinguish three separate periods. The first is not the least fruitful in memories in spite of its short duration. It extends from the dawn of my reason till our dear Mother's departure for Heaven.

God granted me the favor of opening my intelligence at an early age and of imprinting childhood recollections so deeply on my memory that it seems the things I'm about to recount happened only yesterday. Jesus in his love willed, perhaps, that I know the matchless Mother he had given me, but whom his hand hastened to crown in heaven.

God was pleased all through my life to surround me with *love,* and the first memories I have are stamped with smiles and the most tender caresses. But although he placed so much *love* near me, he also sent much love into my little heart, making it warm and affectionate. I loved Mama and Papa very much and showed my tenderness for them in a thousand ways, for I was very expressive. . . .[5]

In the family correspondence we read many stories about the child Thérèse. Her entire family cherished her and treated her with great affection. Here are some excerpts from Zélie Martin to her sister-in-law, Madame Guérin:

Little Thérèse is walking alone since Thursday; she is sweet and darling like a little angel. She has a charming disposition, I see this already. She has such a sweet smile.[6]

From a letter of Madame Martin to her oldest daughters, Marie and Pauline, when they were away at school:

The little baby has just passed her little hand over my face and kissed me. The dear little thing does not want to leave me, she is continually with me; she loves going into the garden very much, but if I am not there, she does not want to remain and cries until someone brings her back to me. . . . I am very happy that she has so much affection for me, but sometimes it is troublesome![7]

From a letter of Marie to her sister, Pauline:

Each morning, [Thérèse] comes here to make her prayer, leaping with joy. If you only knew how full of mischief she is, and yet not silly. I am full of admiration for this little "bouquet." All at home devour her with kisses; she's just a poor little martyr![8]

Oh! everything truly smiled upon me on this earth: I found flowers under each of my steps and my happy disposition contributed much to making life pleasant, but a new period was about to commence for my soul. I had to pass through the crucible of trial and to suffer from my childhood in order to be offered earlier to Jesus. Just as the flowers of spring begin to grow under the snow and to expand in the first rays of the sun, so the little flower whose memories I am writing had to pass through the winter of trial.[9]

II

The Tragic Loss of a Mother

Thérèse's sufferings began at an early age with the death of her mother. At the same time, Thérèse was blessed with an abundance of love from her father and her sisters. Thérèse chose her sister, Pauline, to be her new mother.

All the details of my Mother's illness are still present to me and I recall especially the last weeks she spent on earth. Céline and I were like two poor little exiles, for every morning Mme. Leriche[1] came to get us and brought us to her home where we spent the day. One morning we didn't have time to say our prayers and during the trip Céline whispered: "Should we tell her we didn't say our prayers?" "Oh! yes," I answered. So very timidly Céline told Mme.

Leriche, who said: "Well, my little girls, you will say them," and placing us both in a large room, she left. Céline looked at me and we said: "Oh! This is not like Mama! She always had us say our prayers with her. . . ."

The touching ceremony of the last anointing [of Mama] is also deeply impressed on my mind. I can still see the spot where I was by Céline's side. All five of us were lined up according to age, and Papa was there too, sobbing.

The day of Mama's departure, or the day after, Papa took me in his arms and said: "Come, kiss your poor little Mother for the last time." Without a word I placed my lips on her forehead. I don't recall having cried very much, neither did I speak to anyone about the feelings I experienced. I looked and listened in silence. No one had any time to pay any attention to me, and I saw many things they would have hidden from me. For instance, once I was standing before the lid of the coffin which had been placed upright in the hall. I stopped for a long time gazing at it. Though I'd never seen one before, I understood what it was. I was so little that in spite of Mama's small stature, I had to *raise* my head to take in its full height. It appeared *large* and *dismal*. . . .

The day the Church blessed the mortal remains of our dear mother, now in heaven, God willed to give me another mother on earth. He willed also that I choose her freely.

All five of us were gathered together, looking at each other sadly. Louise[2] was there too, and, seeing Céline and me, she said: "Poor little things, you have no mother any more!" Céline threw her arms around Marie saying: "Well, you will be my Mama!" Accustomed to following Céline's example, I turned instead to you, Mother, and as though the future had torn aside its veil, I threw myself into your arms, crying: "Well, as for me, it's Pauline who will be my Mama!"

As I've already said, it's from the end of this phase in my life that I entered the second period of my existence, the most painful of the three, especially since the entrance into Carmel of the one whom I chose as my second "Mama." This period extends from the age of four and a half to that of fourteen, the time when I found once again my *childhood* character, and entered more and more into the serious side of life.

I must admit, Mother, my happy disposition completely changed after Mama's death. I, once so full of life, became timid and retiring, sensitive to an excessive degree. One look was enough to reduce me to tears, and the only way I was content was to be left alone completely. I could not bear the company of strangers and found my joy only within the intimacy of the family.

And still I continued to be surrounded with the most delicate *tenderness*. Our Father's *very affectionate heart* seemed to be enriched now with a truly maternal love! You and Marie, Mother, were you not *the most tender* and selfless of mothers? Ah! If God had not showered his beneficent *rays* upon his little flower, she could never have accustomed herself to earth, for she was too weak to stand up against the rains and the storms. She needed warmth, a gentle dew, and the springtime breezes. Never were these lacking. Jesus had her find them beneath the snow of trial! [3]

III

A Prophetic Sign

Thérèse describes a mysterious episode or "vision" that took place when she was six years old. This disturbing occurrence caused her much anxiety for years; it was a premonition of her father's suffering in the last five years of his life.

Ah! How joyous were these family feasts! How far I was then from foreseeing the trials awaiting my dear King [1] when seeing him so happy! One day, however, God showed me in a truly extraordinary *vision* the *living* image of the trial he was pleased to prepare for us in advance. [2]

Papa was on a trip for several days and was not expected to return for two more days. It could have been about two or three o'clock in the afternoon; the sun was shining brightly and all nature seemed to be rejoicing. I was all alone at the window of an attic which faced the large garden; I was looking straight ahead, my mind occupied with joyful thoughts, when I saw a man dressed exactly like Papa standing in front of the laundry which was just opposite. The man had the same height and walk as Papa, only he was *much more stooped*. His *head* was covered with a sort of apron of indistinct color and it hid his face. He wore a hat similar to Papa's. I saw him walking at a regular pace along my little garden. Immediately a feeling of supernatural fright invaded my soul, but in an instant I reflected that surely Papa had returned and was hiding to surprise me; then I called out very loudly—"Papa! Papa!"—my voice trembling with emotion. But the mysterious personage, appearing not to hear, continued his steady pace without even turning around. Following him with my eyes, I saw him go toward the grove that divides the wide path in two, and I waited to see him reappear on the other side of the tall trees, but the prophetic vision had vanished! All this lasted but an instant but was engraved so deeply on my heart that today, after fifteen years, it is as present to me as though I were still seeing the vision before my eyes.

Marie was with you, Mother, in a room adjoining the one where I was; hearing me call Papa, she experienced fright also, feeling, as she told me later, that something extraordinary must have happened. Without allowing me to see her emotion, she ran to me and asked what possessed me to call Papa, who was still at Alençon. I told her what I had just seen. To calm me down, Marie said it was no doubt Victoire[3] who hid her head in her apron to frighten me, but when asked about it, Victoire said she hadn't left her kitchen. Besides, I was very sure I'd seen a man and this man had Papa's appearance. Then all three of us went behind the screen of trees, but when we found no mark indicating the passage of anyone, you told me to think no more about it.

It was not within my power to think no more about it. Very often my imagination presented again the mysterious scene I had witnessed. Very often, too, I tried to lift the veil that was hiding its meaning from me because I kept in the bottom of my heart the conviction that this vision had a meaning which was one day to be revealed to me. That day was a long time in coming; but after fourteen years God himself tore away the mysterious veil.

[Later, in Carmel,] I had permission to be with Sister Marie of the Sacred Heart [Thérèse's sister, Marie], and we were talking as always about the things of the other life and our childhood memories. I recalled to her the vision I had seen at the age of six or seven, and all of a sudden, while I was describing the details of the strange scene, we understood simultaneously what it meant. It was indeed *Papa* whom I had seen advancing, bent over with age. It was indeed Papa, who was bearing on his venerable countenance and white hair the symbol of his *glorious* trial.[4] Just as the adorable Face of Jesus was veiled during his Passion, so the face of his faithful servant had to be veiled in the days of his sufferings in order that it might shine in the heavenly Fatherland near its Lord, the Eternal Word! . . .

Ah! Why was it to me that God gave this light? Why did he show such a small child a thing she couldn't understand, a thing which, if she had understood, would have made her die of grief? Why? This is one of the mysteries we shall understand only in heaven and which we shall eternally admire!

How good God really is! How he parcels out trials only according to the strength he gives us. Never, as I've said already, would I have been able to bear even the thought of the bitter pains the future held in store for me. I wasn't even able to think of Papa *dying* without trembling.[5]

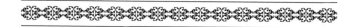

IV

Painful Separations

Thérèse experienced many separations that caused her deep suffering, especially her mother's death and her sisters' entrance into the convent. Pauline's departure from home to enter Carmel was an acutely difficult separation, for Pauline had been Thérèse's adopted "little mother"!

[N]ow I must speak of the sorrowful trial that broke little Thérèse's heart when Jesus took away her dear *Mama*, her tenderly loved *Pauline!* [1]

How [I] suffered when [I] heard dear Pauline speaking one day to Marie about her coming entrance into Carmel. I didn't know what Carmel was, but I understood that Pauline was going to leave me to enter a convent. I understood, too, she *would not wait for me* and I was about to lose my second *Mother!* Ah! How can I express the anguish of my heart! In one instant, I understood what life was; until then, I had never seen it so sad; but it appeared to me in all its reality, and I saw it was nothing but a continual suffering and separation. I shed bitter tears because I did not yet understand the *joy* of sacrifice. I was *weak,* so *weak* that I consider it a great grace to have been able to support a trial that seemed to be far above my strength! If I had learned of my dear Pauline's departure very gently, I would not have suffered as much perhaps, but having heard about it by surprise, it was as if a sword were buried in my heart.

I shall always remember, dear Mother, with what tenderness you consoled me. Then you explained the life of Carmel to me and it seemed so beautiful! When thinking over all you had said, I felt that Carmel was the *desert* where God wanted me to go also to hide myself. I felt this with so much force that there wasn't the least doubt in my heart; it was not the dream of a child led astray but the *certitude* of a divine call; I wanted to go to Carmel not for *Pauline's sake* but for *Jesus alone*. . . .

Finally *October 2* arrived. . . . I still see the spot where I received *Pauline's* last kiss; and then Aunt brought us to Mass, while Papa went to Mount Carmel to offer his *first sacrifice.* The whole family was in tears so that people who saw us coming into the church looked at us in surprise. But it was all the same to me and it didn't prevent me from crying. I believed that if everything crumbled around me, I would have paid no attention whatsoever. I looked up at the beautiful blue skies and was astonished the Sun was shining with such brightness when my soul was flooded with sadness! Perhaps, dear Mother, you find I am exaggerating the pain I was experiencing? I readily admit that it should not have been as great, since I had the hope of finding you again in Carmel; but my soul was FAR from being *mature,* and I was to pass through many crucibles of suffering before attaining the end I so much desired.[2]

Marie's departure from home to enter Carmel was another separation that caused much distress for Thérèse.

I was to pass through many separations; the year, for instance, when I was received as a child of the Blessed Virgin, she took from me my dear Marie, the only support of my soul. It was Marie who guided, consoled, and aided me in the practice of virtue; she was my sole oracle. Pauline, no doubt, had remained well ahead in my heart, but Pauline was far, very far from me! I had suffered martyrdom getting accustomed to living without her, to seeing between me and her impassable walls. But finally I ended up by recognizing the sad reality: Pauline is lost to me, almost in the same manner as if she were dead. She always loved me, prayed for me, but in my eyes *my* dear *Pauline* had become a saint who was no longer able to understand the things of earth. . . . Besides, even when I would have desired to confide my thoughts to her as at Les Buissonnets, I could not have done so, for the visits at the Carmel were only for Marie. Céline and I had permission to come only at the end, just to have the time to break our heart.[3]

Many years later, both older sisters, Marie and Pauline, recall with regret these family visits to Carmel when less attention was paid to Thérèse.

Marie writes: Each week, I used to return to the Carmel as to the spring of all my happiness. Ah! How sorry I am today for not having shared with my little sisters this visit, which I found, however, too short for me. If I had only known that my poor little Thérèse had suffered so much from this! I was far from suspecting it. . . .

Pauline writes: I used to be very sad when Thérèse cried at the end of Marie's visits. But how was I to console her! I was unaware of the abyss of sadness that formed in her soul at my departure. I understand very well now how the five minutes given to her with me could only cause her more anguish. And, then, I was so foolish with all my politeness to my aunt when she came with my cousins!

Céline and Thérèse no longer counted; all my attention was centered on the other side. . . . And yet I believed I was acting well, and that Marie was going to understand me and have my poor little Thérèse understand me, in whose eyes I always used to see tears forming! And a little pout which would show whenever she tried to refrain from crying any more. Ah! Once again, if I had only known![4]

Thérèse continues: And so, in reality, I had only Marie, and she was indispensable to me, so to speak. I told my scruples[5] only to her and was so obedient that my confessor never knew my ugly malady. I told him just the number of sins Marie permitted me to confess, not one more, and could pass as being the least scrupulous soul on earth in spite of the fact that I was scrupulous to the highest degree. Marie knew, then, everything that went on in my soul, and she knew my desires for Carmel. I loved her so much I couldn't live without her.[6]

After entering Carmel, Marie (now known as Sister Marie of the Sacred Heart) wrote to Thérèse:

I don't want my darling to cry like this, but I want her to be good and reasonable. After all, we shouldn't say that today was the last time in her life that she was seeing me! And when we think that on Thursday morning this baby will return for a visit and again on Friday! . . .

See you soon, my love. . . . But I don't want my darling to despair when God has spoiled her *so much . . . so much*. Let her reflect a little on God's treats. That is something which will dry all her tears.

Your little godmother, who loves you.

Marie of the Sacred Heart. [7]

Thérèse describes her sadness over Léonie's departure from home as she made her initial attempt to enter a convent.

[It was on a trip to Alençon] that Léonie made her attempt to enter the Poor Clares. [8] I was saddened by her *extraordinary* entrance, for I loved her very much and I hadn't even the chance to kiss her before her departure. Never will I forget the kindness and embarrassment of this poor little Father of ours when he came to announce that Léonie had already received the habit of the Poor Clares. He found this very strange, just as we did, but he didn't want to say anything when he saw how unhappy Marie was about the matter. . . .

When leaving Alençon I believed she would remain with the Poor Clares, and so it was with a heavy heart I left the *sad* street of *Demi-lune* (half moon). We were only three now and soon our Marie was also to leave. The 15th of October was the day of separation! From the happy and numerous family of Les Buissonnets there remained only the two youngest children. . . . [9]

Léonie, ten years older than Thérèse, was the child who caused most grief for the Martin family, including her mother, who worried about and prayed intensely for her rebellious child. But one day Zélie discovered that their maid had been physically and emotionally abusing and beating Léonie to keep her under her control. Zélie immediately fired the maid and treated Léonie with the greatest gentleness. Freed from this abuse, Léonie changed into a more amiable person.[10] But she continued to struggle throughout her life. After several unsuccessful attempts to enter religious life, she definitively entered the Visitation convent where she lived a humble, holy life until her death at the age of seventy-eight on June 3, 1941.

Two days before Léonie's first departure, Thérèse wrote to her cousin Marie Guérin, and, after teasing her cousin about a dental visit, she speaks of Léonie:

I received your dear little letter just this minute, and I'm still laughing when thinking of all you're telling me. Well, then, you naughty little thing, I must first begin by scolding you. Why did you take your face again to the sculptor [dentist]? He has really done a fine job on it! . . . I was really sorry when I learned your naughty little cheeks had once again taken on the form of a balloon. . . .

This week we're no longer cheerful at Les Buissonnets; it's the last week that Léonie is spending with us. The days are passing by rapidly, and she has only two more days with us.

However, what do you expect, my poor darling? A certain joy is mixed with my sorrow, and I am happy to see dear Léonie finally in her element; yes, I believe that there only will she be happy. In the Visitation, she will find what she is missing in the world. [11]

V

Emotional Trials

Thérèse writes in detail about a mysterious childhood illness she suffered and the cure she received from the Blessed Virgin. Lacking proper medical terminology to explain Thérèse's ailment, the tendency was to attribute it to evil forces. But modern Teresian writers interpret these unusual incidents as a deep psychological trauma, the "separation anxiety" that this highly sensitive child experienced after the death of her mother. It was compounded by Therese's separation from Pauline, her "second mother," when the latter entered the convent. Thérèse and her devout family credited her quick improvement to the Blessed Virgin's miraculous intercession. And in fact, the grace of God had worked within the child Thérèse to help her cope with her sense of abandonment.[1]

It is surprising to see how much my mind developed in the midst of suffering; it developed to such a degree that it wasn't long before I became sick.

The sickness which overtook me [after Pauline had left] certainly came from the demon; infuriated by your entrance into Carmel, he wanted to take revenge on me for the wrong our family was to do him in the future. But he did not know that the sweet Queen of heaven was watching over her fragile little flower, that she *was smiling* on her from her throne in heaven and was preparing to stop the storm the moment her flower was to break without any hope of recovery.

Toward the end of the year, I began to have a constant headache. It didn't cause me much suffering. I was able to pursue my studies and nobody was worried about me. This lasted until Easter, 1883. Papa had gone to Paris with Marie and Léonie, and Aunt [Mme. Guérin] had taken me and Céline with her into her home. One evening Uncle [Isidore Guérin] took me for a walk and spoke about Mama and about past memories with a kindness that touched me profoundly and made me cry. Then he told me I was too softhearted, that I needed a lot of distraction, and he was determined to give us a good time during our Easter vacation. He and Aunt would see to it. That night we were to go to the Catholic Circle meeting, but finding I was too fatigued, Aunt made me go to bed; when I was undressing,

I was seized with a strange trembling. Believing I was cold, Aunt covered me with blankets and surrounded me with hot water bottles. But nothing was able to stop my shaking, which lasted almost all night. Uncle, returning from the meeting with my cousins and Céline, was very much surprised to see me in this state, which he judged to be very serious. He didn't want to say this in order not to frighten Aunt.

He went to get Doctor Notta the next day, and he judged, as did Uncle, that I had a very serious illness and one which had never before attacked a child as young as I. Everybody was puzzled. Aunt was obliged to keep me at her home, and she took care of me with a truly *maternal* solicitude. When Papa returned from Paris with my older sisters, Aimée[2] met them at the door with such a sad face that Marie believed I had died. This sickness was not "unto death," but like that of Lazarus it was to give glory to God. And God was glorified by the admirable resignation of my poor little *Father*, who thought his *"little girl was going crazy or was about to die."* God was glorified too by *Marie's* resignation! Ah! How she suffered because of me, and how grateful I am to her for the care she lavished upon me with such unselfishness . . . .[3]

. . . Pauline's taking of the habit was approaching. They avoided talking about it in my presence, knowing the pain I felt, but I spoke about it often and said I would be well enough to go and see my dear Pauline. . . . Ah! How *beautiful that day* was, even in the midst of my dark trial, but it passed by quickly. Soon I had to climb into the carriage which took me to Les Buissonnets, far from Pauline and from my beloved Carmel. When we reached home, they put me to bed in spite of my assurances that I was perfectly cured and needed no further attention. Alas! My trial was only commencing! The next day I had another attack similar to the first, and the sickness became so grave that, according to human calculations, I wasn't to recover from it. I can't describe this strange sickness, but I'm now convinced it was the work of the devil. For a long time after my cure, however, I believed I had become ill on purpose and this was a *real martyrdom* for my soul.

I told Marie this and with her usual *kindness* she reassured me. I told it too in confession and my confessor tried to calm me, saying it was not possible to pretend illness to the extent that I had been ill. God, willing no doubt to purify and especially to *humble me*, left me with this *interior martyrdom* until my entrance into Carmel, where the *Father* of our souls, as with the wave of his hand, removed all my doubts. Since then I am perfectly calm.

It isn't surprising that I feared having appeared sick when I wasn't sick in reality because I said and did things that were not in my mind. I appeared to be almost always delirious, saying things that had no meaning. And still I am *sure* that I *was not deprived of the use of my reason for one single instant.* I often appeared to be in a faint, not making the slightest movement, and then I would have permitted any-one to do anything he wished, even to kill me, and yet I heard everything that was said around me and can still remember everything. Once it happened that for a long time I was without the power to open my eyes and to open them an instant when I was alone.

I believe the devil had received an *external* power over me but was not allowed to approach my soul nor my mind except to inspire me with very great *fears* of certain things, for example, very simple remedies they tried in vain to make me accept. But although God permitted the devil to come near me, He also sent me visible angels. Marie was always by my bedside, taking care of me and consoling me with a mother's tenderness. Never did she show the slight-est sign of annoyance, and still I gave her a lot of trouble, not even allowing her to be away from me. She had to go and eat her meals with Papa, but I never stopped calling her all the time she was away. Victoire, who was taking care of me, was at times obliged to go and get my dear "Mama" as I was calling her. When Marie wanted to go out, it had to be either to attend Mass or to go to see *Pauline*, and then I said nothing.

Uncle and Aunt were very good to me; dear little Aunt came every day to visit me and brought a thousand goodies. Other friends of the family came to visit me also, but I begged Marie to tell them I wanted no visits. It displeased me *to "see people seated around my bed LIKE A ROW OF ONIONS, looking at me as though I were a strange beast."* The only visit I liked was that of Uncle and Aunt.[4]

A miracle was necessary [for my cure] and it was our Lady of Victories who worked it. One Sunday during the Novena of Masses,[5] Marie went into the garden, leaving me with Léonie who was reading near the window. After a few moments I began calling in a low tone: "Mama, Mama." Léonie, accustomed to hearing me always calling out like this, didn't pay any attention. This lasted a long time, and then I called her much louder. Marie finally returned. I saw her enter, but I cannot say I recognized her and continued to call her in a louder tone: "Mama." *I was suffering very much* from this forced and inexplicable struggle and Marie was suffering perhaps even more than I. After some futile attempts to show me she was by my side, Marie knelt down near my bed with Léonie and Céline. Turning to the Blessed Virgin and praying with the fervor of a mother begging for the life of her child, *Marie* obtained what she wanted.

Finding no help on earth, poor little Thérèse had also turned toward the Mother of heaven, and prayed with all her heart that she take pity on her. All of a sudden the Blessed Virgin appeared *beautiful* to me, *so beautiful* that never had I seen anything so attractive; her face was suffused with an ineffable benevolence and tenderness, but what penetrated to the very depths of my soul was the *"ravishing smile of the Blessed Virgin."* At that instant, all my pain disappeared, and two large tears glistened on my eyelashes, and flowed down my cheeks silently, but they were tears of unmixed joy. Ah! I thought, the Blessed Virgin smiled at me, how happy I am, but never will I tell anyone for my *happiness would then disappear.* Without any effort I lowered my eyes, and I saw Marie who was looking down at me lovingly; she seemed moved and appeared to surmise the favor the Blessed Virgin had given me. Ah! It was really to her, to her touching prayers that I owed the grace of the Queen of heaven's *smile.* Seeing my gaze fixed on the Blessed Virgin, she cried out: "Thérèse is cured!" [6]

During this illness, Pauline wrote several letters full of warmth and affection to encourage Thérèse. After the cure, Pauline sent this note:

What a joy to see you well! How good the Blessed Virgin really is! I offered her your beautiful bouquet, and she seemed to be all radiant with her little daughter's flowers. . . . Along with the flowers, I expressed a big "thanks," which was as tender as it was big, and I begged her to continue her work and to complete it soon.

Poor darling, how eager I am to see your little face so dear to my heart. I can see it from here, that's true, but for sometime my telescope is no longer any good; when you were so sick, I let a tear fall on the lens and suddenly it became blurred.

Well, the Blessed Virgin keeps us together under her mantle; she is watching over us in her heart, blessing us, loving us and caressing us with the same hand! . . .

Adieu! Let us love the Blessed Virgin, let us love her; she is a Mother, and beneath her glance, beneath her hand, the little bark of her heart is safe and is sailing peacefully toward heaven.

I kiss your little bark, my cherub; always keep at the bottom of its hold the love I know you have for me. I need it just as a little mother needs to be paid in return for the love she has for her child.[7]

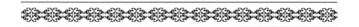

VI

Illness of an Aging Parent

*In the last five years of his life, Louis Martin suffered an ill-
ness marked by physical and psychological elements severe
enough to require hospitalization in a mental health facility. The
entire Martin family suffered greatly, as expressed in their letters.
Louis Martin himself, at times well aware of his condition, suffered with a sense of faithful resignation, deep humility,
prayerfulness, and abandonment to God's will.*

How merciful is the way God has guided me. *Never* has
he given me the desire for anything which he has not given
me, and even his bitter chalice seemed delightful to me.

After those beautiful festivities of the month of May,
namely, the Profession and taking of the Veil of our dear

Marie, the *oldest* in the family being crowned on her *wedding day* [1] by the *youngest*, we had to be visited by trial. The preceding year, in May, Papa was seized with a paralytic stroke in the limbs and we were greatly disturbed. But the strong character of my dear King soon took control and our fears disappeared. However, more than once during the trip to Rome we noticed that he easily grew tired and wasn't as cheerful as usual. What I noticed especially was the progress he was making in perfection. He had succeeded, like St. Francis de Sales, in overcoming his natural impetuosity to such an extent that he appeared to have the most gentle nature in the world. The things of earth seemed hardly to touch him, he easily surmounted contradictions, and God was *flooding* him with *consolations*. . . .

It was time that such a faithful servant receive the reward of his works, and it was right that his wages resemble those which God gave to the King of heaven, his only Son. Papa had just made a donation to God of an *altar,* and it was he who was chosen as victim to be offered with the Lamb without spot. You are aware, dear Mother, of our bitter sufferings during the month of June, and especially June 24, 1888. [2] These memories are too deeply engraved in the bottom of our hearts to require any mention in writing. O Mother! How we suffered! And this was still only the *beginning* of the trial. [3]

Thérèse wrote to her father on November 25, 1888:

Dear little Father,

Your Queen is thinking of you continually, and she is praying all day long for her King. I am very happy in the nest of Carmel, and I no longer desire anything on earth, except to see my dear King entirely cured, but I know why God is sending us this trial; it is so that we win his beautiful heaven. He knows that our dear Father is all that we love most on this earth, but he knows, too, that it is necessary to suffer to gain eternal life, and it is for this that he is trying us in all that we hold most dear.

. . . Is there anyone whom God loves more on this earth than my dear little Father? . . . Really, I cannot believe it! . . . Today, at least, he is giving us the proof that I am not wrong since God always tries those whom he loves. . . .

Adieu, dear King. Your Queen rejoices when thinking of the day when she will reign with YOU in the beautiful and only true *kingdom* of heaven.[4]

The time for my reception of the habit had arrived. . . . Against all expectation, our dear Father recovered from his second attack, and the Bishop set the ceremony for January 10. . . . The celebration . . . was wonderful. The most beautiful, the most attractive flower of all was my dear King; never had he looked so handsome, so *dignified*. Everybody admired him. This was really his day of *triumph* and it was to be his last celebration on this earth. *He had now given all his children to God, for Céline, too, had confided her vocation to him.*[5] He had *wept tears of joy,* and had gone with her to thank him who "bestowed such honor on him by taking all his children."[6]

January 10, as I have just said, was my King's day of triumph. I compare it to the entry of Jesus into Jerusalem on the day of the palms. Like that of our Divine Master, Papa's glory of *a day* was followed by a painful passion and this passion was not his alone. Just as the sufferings of Jesus pierced his Mother's heart with a sword of sorrow, so our hearts experienced the sufferings of the one we cherished most tenderly on earth. I recall that in the month of June, 1888, at the moment of our first trials, I said: "I am suffering very much, but I feel I can still bear greater trials." I was not thinking then of the ones reserved for me. I didn't know that on February 12, a month after my reception of the habit, our dear Father would drink the *most bitter* and *most humiliating* of all chalices.[7]

Sister Agnes of Jesus (Pauline) wrote the following about this trial: "Outside the monastery, many persons made us responsible for this misfortune, caused, they said, by his extreme sorrow, especially when Thérèse entered the Carmel."[8]

A particularly painful incident took place due to M. Martin's hallucinations; these eventually led to his hospitalization in the

Bon Sauveur (Good Savior) hospital, a mental health center in Caen. Céline explains the incident in a letter to a friend:

The doctor at the establishment told us that it was a general paralysis, the whole nervous system was attacked; he believes that the time will come when all his strength will be so weakened that we shall be able to take him home and take care of him until his last breath; this hope gives me courage. It is very sad that the paralysis settled in his brain, otherwise we would still have our very much-loved Father at home. He is incredibly good; he was far from wanting to do us any harm with his revolver; on the contrary, he wanted to defend us. In his imagination, he was seeing frightful things, slaughter, battles; he was hearing the sounds of cannon and the drum. I tried in vain to correct his mistake. An attempt at robbery in the town served only to confirm him in his ideas, so he took his revolver and wanted to carry it on him in case of danger, for he said, "I would not want to harm even a cat." In fact, I don't believe that he would have made use of it; it was just an idea that was passing and it would have vanished. Perhaps they should have waited before acting, and should have tried ways of taking it away from him, for he was so good, so gentle; he used to kiss us with such tenderness! [9]

Isidore Guérin, instead, recognized the seriousness of the situation and arranged for M. Martin's hospitalization. The exact details of this are not clear. Here is a fragment of a letter from Céline to her sisters: "Léonie and I were mute, we kept silent the whole time; we were crushed, broken. It seemed to me that my heart was bleeding and that it had a large wound . . ." [10]

A week after the incident, Céline informed her sisters in Carmel:

The Sister [at Bon Sauveur] said to him [M. Martin] that he was rendering them a great service by bringing back the fallen-away patients to God. "You are an apostle," she told him. "That's true," answered dear little Father, "but I would prefer to be an apostle elsewhere; however, since it is God's will! I believe it is to break down my pride." If you only knew, dear little sisters, how these words struck me to the heart. I think Papa is so holy! . . . But it was when I saw him go back inside, the moment when the door was shut on him again that my heart was torn. He is so good! . . . [11]

The following day, Thérèse responded to Céline's letter:

Ah! Dear little sister, far from complaining to Jesus about the cross he is sending us, I cannot understand the *infinite* love that has drawn him to treat us in this way . . . . Our dear Father must be much loved by Jesus to have to suffer this way, but don't you find that the misfortune that is striking him is really the complement of his beautiful life? . . . I feel . . . that I am speaking real follies to you, but it does not matter. I still think very many other things about the love of Jesus which are perhaps much stronger than what I am saying to you . . . . What a joy to be humbled; it is the only thing that makes saints! . . . Can we doubt now the will of Jesus concerning our souls? . . . Life is only a *dream,* and soon we shall wake up, and what joy . . . the greater our sufferings are the more infinite will be our glory . . . . Oh, let us not lose the trial that Jesus is sending us, it is a gold mine to be exploited. Are we going to miss the chance? . . .[12]

From Céline to her sisters in Carmel:

Sister Costard [at the hospital] takes care of Papa simply as though he were her father; yesterday she was crying when she was giving me information about him: "You see, it's heartbreaking to see this handsome patriarch in such a condition; we are sad, deeply pained, and our staff is dismayed. In the short time that he has been here, he has made himself loved, and, then, there is something so venerable about him! He bears no ordinary stamp. . . . We can see that it is a trial; it doesn't suit him to have this illness, and this makes it all the more distressing!"

This good religious kept repeating: "There is something so venerable about him!" Oh! how true this is. . . .

Dear sisters, Papa will certainly have no purgatory in the other world, but these sorrows are so sharp for us that they can, I think, bring about changes in our souls that will make us saints. I don't believe the saints had harder trials . . . .[13]

The other day, Papa said to the doctor: "I had always been accustomed to commanding, and I see myself reduced to obeying; I never had any humiliations in my life, and I needed one." The doctor answered: "Well, then, this one can count!"[14]

. . . Words cannot express our anguish, and I'm not going to attempt to describe it. One day, in heaven, we shall love talking to one another about our *glorious* trials; don't we already feel happy for having suffered them? Yes, Papa's three years of martyrdom appear to me as the most lovable, the most fruitful of my life; I wouldn't exchange them for all the ecstasies and revelations of the saints . . . . O dear Mother! how sweet our great trial was since from our hearts came only sighs of love and gratitude! We were no longer walking in the way of perfection, we were flying, all five of us. The two poor little exiles of Caen, while still in the world, were no longer of it.[15]

Thérèse wrote to Céline:

Let us suffer the bitter pain. . . . (Jesus suffered in *sadness!* . . .) And still we would like to suffer generously, grandly! . . . Céline! What an illusion! . . . We'd never want to fall? . . . What does it matter, my Jesus, if I fall at each moment; I *see* my weakness through this and this is a great gain for me. . . . *You can see* through this what I can do and now you will be more tempted to carry me in your arms . . . . If you do not do it, it is because this pleases you to see me *on the ground.* . . . Then I am not going to be disturbed, but I shall always stretch out my arms suppliant and filled with love! . . . I cannot believe that you would abandon me! . . .[16]

After three years at Bon Sauveur, M. Martin returned to his family. He died on July 29, 1894, after suffering a stroke in May and a heart attack in June.

Céline wrote to her sisters to give them the news of their father's death:

Dear little sisters,

Papa is in heaven! . . . I received his last breath, I closed his eyes. . . . His handsome face took on immediately an expression of beatitude, of such profound calm! Tranquility was painted on his features. . . . He expired so gently at fifteen minutes after eight.

My poor heart was broken at the supreme moment; a flood of tears bathed his bed. But at heart I was joyful because of his happiness, after the terrible martyrdom he endured and which we shared with him. . . .[17]

Thérèse continues with her memories:

Last year, July 29, God broke the bonds of his incomparable servant and called him to his eternal reward; at the same time he broke those which still held his dear fiancée [Céline] in the world because she had accomplished her mission. Having been given the office *of representing us all* with our father whom we so tenderly loved, she had accomplished this mission just like an angel. And angels don't remain on earth once they've fulfilled God's will, for they return immediately to him, and this is why they're represented with wings. Our angel also spread her white wings; she was ready to fly *far away* to find Jesus, but he made her fly *close by*. He was content with simply accepting the great sacrifice which was very painful for little Thérèse. Her Céline had kept a secret hidden from her for *two full years*. Ah, how Céline herself had suffered because of this! Finally, from heaven my dear King, who never liked stragglers when he was still with us on earth, hastened to arrange Céline's muddled affairs, and she joined us on September 14![18]

Céline joined her sisters in Carmel a month and a half after M. Martin's death. In August 1894 Thérèse wrote a "remembering" prayer/poem. Here is an excerpt that includes the five verses referring to each daughter:

Prayer of a Child of a Saint [19]

Remember your beloved Marie,
Your eldest daughter, the dearest to your heart.
Remember that she filled your life
With her love, charm, and happiness . . .
For God you gave up her sweet presence,
And you blessed the hand that offered suffering to you . . .

O! your Diamond
Always more sparkling
Remember! . . .

Remember your fine bright pearl [Pauline],
Whom you knew as a weak and timid lamb.
See her filled with divine strength
And leading Carmel's flock.
She has become the Mother of your other children.
O Papa! Come guide her who is so dear to you! . . .

And without leaving Heaven
Your little Carmel
Remember! . . .

Remember the ardent prayer
You made for your third child [Léonie].
God granted it, for on earth she is
Like her sisters, a very brilliant beautiful Lily.

The Visitation hides her from the eyes of the world,
But she loves Jesus, she is flooded with his peace.
>   Her ardent desires
>   And all her sighs
>   Remember! . . .

Remember your dear Céline,
Who was like an angel from Heaven for you
When a glance from the Divine Face
Came to test you by a glorious choice . . . .
You reign in Heaven . . . . Her task is complete.
Now she gives her life to Jesus . . . .
>   Protect your child
>   Who repeats so often
>   Remember! . . .

Remember your little queen [Thérèse],
The orphan of Bérésina.[20]
Remember her uncertain steps.
It was always your hand that guided her.
O Papa! Remember that in the days of her childhood
You wanted to keep her innocence for God alone! . . .
>   And her blonde hair
>   That delighted your eyes
>   Remember! . . .

VII

Love and Abandonment

Thérèse reflects on her vocation to love:

When the difficulties seemed insurmountable one day, I said to Jesus during my act of thanksgiving: "You know, my God, how much I want to know whether Papa went *straight to heaven;* I am not asking you to speak to me, but give me a sign. If Sister Aimée of Jesus consents to Céline's entrance [into Carmel] or places no obstacle to it, this will be an answer that Papa went *straight to you."* This Sister, as you are aware, dear Mother, found we were already too many with three, and she didn't want another of our family to be admitted. But God who holds the hearts of his creatures in his hand, inclining them to do his will, changed this Sister's dispositions. The first one to meet me after my thanksgiving was Sister Aimée, and she called me over to her with a friendly smile and told me to come up with her to your cell. She spoke to me about Céline and there were tears in her eyes. Ah! How many things I have to thank Jesus for; he answers all my requests!

And now I have no other desire except *to love* Jesus unto folly. My childish desires have all flown away. I still love to adorn the Infant Jesus' altar with flowers, but ever since he has given me the *Flower* I desired, my *dear Céline,* I desire no other; she is the one I offer him as my most delightful bouquet.

Neither do I desire any longer suffering or death, and still I love them both; it is *love* alone that attracts me, however. I desired them for a long time; I possessed suffering and believed I had touched the shores of heaven, that the little flower would be gathered in the springtime of her life. Now, abandonment alone guides me. I have no other compass! I can no longer ask for anything with fervor except the accomplishment of God's will in my soul without any creature being able to set obstacles in the way. I can speak these words of the Spiritual Canticle of St. John of the Cross:

> . . . Now I occupy my soul
> and all my energy in his service;

I no longer tend the herd,

nor have I any other work

now that my every act is LOVE . . . .

How sweet is the way of *love*, dear Mother. True, one can fall or commit infidelities, but, knowing *how to draw profit from everything*, love quickly consumes everything that can be displeasing to Jesus; it leaves nothing but a humble and profound peace in the depths of the heart.[1]

The Night of Faith

Along with the unbearable pain of her illness (tuberculosis), Thérèse was tried even further by a severe spiritual crisis. She experienced temptations against the faith, and the lack of spiritual consolation—a true dark night of the soul—that lasted until her death.

Dear Mother,[1] you know well that God has deigned to make me pass through many types of trials. I have suffered very much since I was on earth, but, if in my childhood I suffered with sadness, it is no longer in this way that I suffer. It is with joy and peace. I am truly happy to suffer. O Mother, you must know all the secrets of my soul in order not to smile when you read these lines, for is there a soul less tried than my own if one judges by appearances? Ah! If the trial I am suffering for a year now appeared to the eyes of anyone, what astonishment would be felt![2]

Dear mother, you know about this trial; I am going to speak to you about it, however, for I consider it as a great grace I received during your office as Prioress.

God granted me, last year, the consolation of observing the fast during Lent in all its rigor. Never had I felt so strong, and this strength remained with me until Easter. On Good Friday, however, Jesus wished to give me the hope of going to see him soon in heaven. Oh! How sweet this memory really is! After remaining at the Tomb until midnight, I returned to our cell, but I had scarcely laid my head upon the pillow when I felt something like a bubbling stream mounting to my lips. I didn't know what it was, but I thought that perhaps I was going to die and my soul was flooded with joy. However, as our lamp was extinguished, I told myself I would have to wait until the morning to be certain of my good fortune, for it seemed to me that it was blood I had coughed up. The morning was not long in coming; upon awakening, I thought immediately of the joyful thing that I had to learn, and so I went over to the window. I was able to see that I was not mistaken. Ah! My soul was filled with a great consolation; I was interiorly persuaded that Jesus, on the anniversary of his own death, wanted to have me hear his first call. *It was like a sweet and distant murmur that announced the Bridegroom's arrival.*

It was with great fervor that I assisted at Prime and the Chapter of Pardons. I was in a rush to see my turn come in order to be able, when asking pardon from you, to confide my hope and my happiness to you, dear Mother; however, I added that I was not suffering in the least (which was true) and I begged you, Mother, to give me nothing special. In fact, I had the consolation of spending Good Friday just as I desired. Never did Carmel's austerities appear so delightful to me; the hope of going to heaven soon transported me with joy. When the evening of that blessed day arrived, I had to go to my rest; but just as on the preceding night, good Jesus gave me the same sign that my entrance into eternal life was not far off.

At this time I was enjoying such a living faith, such a clear *faith*, that the thought of heaven made up all my happiness, and I was unable to believe there were really impious people who had no faith. I believed they were actually speaking against their own inner convictions when they denied the existence of heaven, that beautiful heaven where God himself wanted to be their Eternal Reward. During those very joyful days of the Easter season, Jesus made me feel that there were really souls who have no faith, and who, through the abuse of grace, lost this precious treasure, the source of the only real and pure joys. He permitted my soul to be invaded by the thickest darkness, and that the thought of heaven, up until then so sweet to me, be no longer anything but the cause of struggle and torment. This trial was to last not a few days or a few weeks, it was not to be extinguished until the hour set by God himself and this hour has not yet come. I would like to be able to express what I feel, but alas! I believe this is impossible. One would have to travel through this dark tunnel to understand its darkness. I will try to explain it by a comparison.

I imagine I was born in a country that is covered in thick fog. I never had the experience of contemplating the joyful appearance of nature flooded and transformed by the brilliance of the sun. It is true that from childhood I heard people speak of these marvels, and I know the country I am living in is not really my true fatherland, and there is another I must long for without ceasing. This is not simply a story invented by someone living in the sad country where I am, but it is a reality, for the King of the Fatherland of the bright sun actually came and lived for thirty-three years in the land of darkness. Alas! the darkness did not understand that this Divine King was the Light of the world. . . .

I was saying that the certainty of going away one day far from the sad and dark country had been given me from the day of my childhood. I did not believe this only because I heard it from persons much more knowledgeable than I, but I felt in the bottom of my heart real longings for this most beautiful country. . . . Then suddenly the fog that surrounds me becomes more dense; it penetrates my soul and envelops it in such a way that it is impossible to discover within it the sweet image of my Fatherland; everything has disappeared! When I want to rest my heart fatigued by the darkness that surrounds it by the memory of the luminous country after which I aspire, my torment redoubles; it seems to me that the darkness, borrowing the voice of sinners, says mockingly to me: "you are dreaming about the light, about a fatherland embalmed in the sweetest perfumes; you are dreaming about the *eternal* possession of the Creator of all these marvels; you believe that one day you will walk out of this fog that surrounds you! Advance, advance; rejoice in death which will give you not what you hope for but a night still more profound, the night of nothingness."

Dear Mother, the image I wanted to give you of the darkness that obscures my soul is as imperfect as a sketch is to the model; however, I don't want to write any longer about it; I fear I might blaspheme; I fear even that I have already said too much.

Ah! May Jesus pardon me if I have caused him any pain, but he knows very well that while I do not have the *joy of faith,* I am trying to carry out its works at least. I believe I have made more acts of faith in this past year than all through my whole life. At each new occasion of combat, when my enemies provoke me, I conduct myself bravely. Knowing it is cowardly to enter into a duel, I turn my back on my adversaries without deigning to look them in the face; but I run toward my Jesus. I tell him I am ready to shed my blood to the last drop to profess my faith in the existence of *heaven.* I tell him, too, I am happy not to enjoy this beautiful heaven on this earth so that he will open it for all eternity to poor unbelievers. Also, in spite of this trial which has taken away *all my joy,* I can nevertheless cry out: *"You have given me DELIGHT, O Lord, in ALL your doings"* (Ps 91:5). For is there a *joy* greater than that of suffering out of love for you? The more interior the suffering is and the less apparent to the eyes of creatures, the more it rejoices you, O my God! But if my suffering was really unknown to you, which is impossible, I would still be happy to have it, if through it I could prevent or make reparation for one single sin against *faith.*

My dear Mother, I may perhaps appear to you to be exaggerating my trial. In fact, if you are judging according to the sentiments I express in my little poems composed this year, I must appear to you as a soul filled with consolations and one for whom the veil of faith is almost torn aside; and yet it is no longer a veil for me, it is a wall which reaches right up to the heavens and covers the starry firmament. When I sing of the happiness of heaven and of the eternal possession of God, I feel no joy in this, for I sing simply what I WANT TO BELIEVE. It is true that at times a very small ray of the sun comes to illumine my darkness, and then the trial ceases for *an instant,* but afterward the memory of this ray, instead of causing me joy, makes my darkness even more dense.

Never have I felt before this, dear Mother, how sweet and merciful the Lord really is, for he did not send me this trial until the moment I was capable of bearing it. A little earlier I believe it would have plunged me into a state of discouragement. Now it is taking away everything that could be a natural satisfaction in my desire for heaven. Dear Mother, it seems to me now that nothing could prevent me from flying away, for I no longer have any great desires except that of loving to the point of dying of love.[3]

Mother Agnes, Thérèse's older sister Pauline, recorded the brief last conversations of her dying sister. Pauline wrote:

One evening in the infirmary, [Thérèse] was drawn to confide her troubles to me more than she usually did. She had not yet opened up in this way on this subject. Up until then, I had known her trial of faith only vaguely:

Thérèse said to her:

If you only knew what frightful thoughts obsess me! Pray very much for me in order that I do not listen to the devil who wants to persuade me about so many lies. It's the reasoning of the worst materialists which is imposed upon my mind: Later, unceasingly making new advances, science will explain everything naturally; we shall have the absolute reason for everything that exists and that still remains a problem, because there remain very many things to be discovered, etc., etc.

. . . O little Mother, must one have thoughts like this when one loves God so much!

Finally, I offer up these very great pains to obtain the light of faith for poor unbelievers, for all those who separate themselves from the Church's beliefs.

Pauline notes: She added that she never reasoned with these thoughts:

I undergo them under duress, but while undergoing them I never cease making acts of faith.[4]

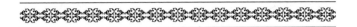

IX

Final Illness

Saint Thérèse does not speak much about her final illness in Story of a Soul. *Most of the information from her last months comes from the correspondence between the Martin and Guérin families, and in particular from notes that her sisters Pauline, Marie, and Céline jotted down when they cared for Thérèse. By April 1896 signs of her tuberculosis were beginning to show. Her condition worsened about a year later, and she progressively declined until her death on September 30, 1897.*

Ever since I was young, God gave me the feeling that I would die young.[1]

Saturday, July 17, at 2:00 A.M., she coughed up blood:

I feel that I'm about to enter into my rest. But I feel especially that my mission is about to begin, my mission of making God loved as I love him, of giving my little way to souls. If God answers my desires, my heaven will be spent on earth until the end of the world. Yes, I want to spend my heaven in doing good on earth. This isn't impossible, since from the bosom of the beatific vision, the angels watch over us.

I can't make heaven a feast of rejoicing; I can't rest as long as there are souls to be saved. But when the angel will have said: "Time is no more!" then I will take my rest; I'll be able to rejoice, because the number of the elect will be complete and because all will have entered into joy and repose. My heart beats with joy at this thought.[2]

From a letter of their cousin, Sister Marie of the Eucharist, to her father (M. Guérin) about three months before Thérèse died:

I come to give you news of your little Queen's health. The news is more and more disturbing. Yesterday, Dr. De Cornière came twice during the day. He's terribly worried. . . . Today, she is perhaps a little better. The fever has dropped, but she feels very weak and isn't able to raise her hand to her mouth, it just falls by her side. . . .

When we visit her, we find her very much changed, very emaciated, but she's always calm, always ready to joke. . . . Loving God the way she does, how well received she'll be up there in heaven. She'll go straight to heaven, that is certain. When we spoke to her about purgatory for ourselves, she said: *"Oh! How you grieve me! You do a great injury to God in believing you're going to purgatory. When we love, we can't go there."*

To mention the state the community is in, there are tears, sobs, and grief on all sides. Mother Agnes of Jesus is to be admired for her courage and resignation; our Mother Prioress has a real motherly tenderness towards all of us in the midst of the greatest of pains, for Sister Thérèse of the Child Jesus was her greatest treasure.[3]

From Sister Geneviève (Céline) to her cousin, Madame La Néele (Jeanne):

Dear little Jeanne,

Your letter touched me very much. You can understand all I have to suffer. It's true that the older ones [Marie and Pauline] could call themselves our mothers, but we two, the two little ones, we formed one, we had never left each other, our souls, our hearts were beating in unison. Now God is about to take her from this exile, and am I to argue with him over her? Oh! no, our dear little angel has often repeated to us the words of our Lord: "Nevertheless I tell you the truth: it is to your advantage that I go away, for if I do not go away, the Counselor will not come to you; but if I go, I will send him to you" (Jn 16:7). She told me too: *"You recall the two little bluebirds I bought you at Le Havre, how they never sang; then when the first one died, the second began to warble, and it sang its most beautiful song and afterwards died."* When my dear Thérèse has died, I shall try to offer to the Lord a song which I haven't sung as yet; the bitterness of this suffering will provide me with a new voice.

But I'll stop here; I can say no more because my grief is too great. My little companion, my dear sister, my friend, my little better half, this is the one who is leaving. I can't understand what will happen; it will make a void in my spirit. It's the keenest blow that could touch me, and perhaps it will be the last. . . .[4]

Thérèse to her uncle and aunt, M. and Mme. Guérin:

I am very happy to prove to you that your little Thérèse has not yet left the exile, for I know this will please you. However, it seems to me, dear relatives, your joy will be greater still when, instead of reading a few lines written with a trembling hand, you will feel my soul near your own. Ah! I am certain God will allow me to pour out his favors lavishly upon you, my little sister Jeanne, and her dear Francis. . . .

My sisters, I know, have spoken to you about my cheerfulness. It is true that I am like a finch except when I have a fever; fortunately, it usually comes to visit me only at night during the hour when finches sleep, their heads hidden beneath their wings. I would not be so cheerful as I am if God were not showing me that the only joy on earth is to accomplish his will. One day, I believe I am at the door of heaven because of the puzzled look of Doctor De Cornière, and the next day he goes off very happy, saying: "Here you are on the road to recovery." What I think (the little *milk baby*) is that I shall not be cured, but that I could *drag on* for a long time still. *A Dieu,* dear relatives, I shall speak to you only in heaven about my affection, as long as I *shall drag on,* my pencil will not be able to express it.[5]

From Thérèse's letter to Father Adolphe Roulland, a missionary:

I really count on not remaining inactive in heaven. My desire is to work still for the Church and for souls. I am asking God for this and I am certain he will answer me. Are not the angels continually occupied with us without their ever ceasing to see the divine Face and to lose themselves in the ocean of Love without shores? Why would Jesus not allow me to imitate them?

. . . What attracts me to the homeland of heaven is the Lord's call, the hope of loving him finally as I have so much desired to love him, and the thought that I shall be able to make him loved by a multitude of souls who will bless him eternally.[6]

Lovingly cared for by her own sisters, and supported prayerfully by the community during her last days on earth, Thérèse died at 7:00 P.M. on September 30, 1897.

From Mother Agnes of Jesus to M. and Mme. Guérin, and Léonie:

Our Angel is in heaven. She gave up her last sigh at seven, while pressing her crucifix to her heart, saying: "Oh! I love you!" She had just raised her eyes to heaven, what was she seeing!!! [7]

X

Source of Strength

Prayer and love synthesize Saint Thérèse's brief and holy life. May her example help all Christians grow in the same sentiments.

I understand and I know from experience that: *"The kingdom of God is within you"* (Lk 17:21). Jesus has no need of books or teachers to instruct souls; he teaches without the noise of words. Never have I heard him speak, but I feel that he is within me at each moment; he is guiding and inspiring me with what I must say and do. I find just when I need them certain lights that I had not seen until then, and it isn't most frequently during my hours of prayer that these are most abundant, but rather in the midst of my daily occupations.[1]

O Jesus, allow me in my boundless gratitude to say to you that your *love reaches unto folly.* In the presence of this folly, how can you not desire that my heart leap toward you? How can my confidence, then, have any limits? Ah! The saints have committed their *follies* for you, and they have done great things because they are eagles.[2]

How great is the power of *Prayer!* One could call it a Queen who has at each instant free access to the King and who is able to obtain whatever she asks. To be heard it is not necessary to read from a book some beautiful formula composed for the occasion. If this were the case, alas, I would have to be pitied! Outside the *Divine Office,* which I am very unworthy to recite, I do not have the courage to force myself to search out *beautiful* prayers in books. There are so many of them it really gives me a headache! And each prayer is more *beautiful* than the others. I cannot recite them all and not knowing which to choose, I do like children who do not know how to read, I say very simply to God what I wish to say, without composing beautiful sentences, and he always understands me. For me, *prayer* is an aspiration of the heart, it is a simple glance directed to heaven, it is a cry of gratitude and love in the midst of trial as well as joy; finally, it is something great, supernatural, which expands my souls and unites me to Jesus.[3]

Sometimes when my mind is in such a great aridity that it is impossible to draw forth one single thought to unite me with God, I *very slowly* recite an "Our Father" and then the angelic salutation [the Hail Mary]; then these prayers give me great delight; they nourish my soul much more than if I had recited them precipitately a hundred times.

The Blessed Virgin shows me she is not displeased with me, for she never fails to protect me as soon as I invoke her. If some disturbance overtakes me, some embarrassment, I turn very quickly to her and as the most tender of Mothers she always takes care of my interests.[4]

Living on Love is giving without limit
Without claiming any wages here below.
Ah! I give without counting, truly sure
That when one loves, one does not keep count! . . .
Overflowing with tenderness, I have given everything,
To his Divine Heart . . . . lightly I run.
I have nothing left but my only wealth:
    Living on Love.

Living on Love is banishing every fear,
Every memory of past faults.
I see no imprint of my sins.
In a moment love has burned everything . . . .
Divine Flame, O very sweet Blaze!

I make my home in your hearth.
In your fire I gladly sing:
    "I live on Love! . . ."

Dying of Love is what I hope for.
When I shall see my bonds broken,
My God will be my Great Reward.
I don't desire to possess other goods.
I want to be set on fire with his Love.
I want to see him, to unite myself to him forever.
That is my heaven . . . that is my destiny:
    Living on Love!!! . . .[5]

Notes

Foreword

1. John Clarke, trans., *Letters of St. Thérèse of Lisieux,* vol. 1 *(1877–1890)* (Washington, D.C.: ICS Publications, 1982), 113.

2. John Clarke, trans., *Letters of St. Thérèse of Lisieux,* vol. 2 *(1890–1897)* (Washington, D.C.: ICS Publications, 1988), 1028.

3. John Clarke, trans., *Story of a Soul: The Autobiography of St. Thérèse of Lisieux,* 3rd ed. (Washington, D.C.: ICS Publications, 1996), 195.

4. Clarke, *Letters,* vol. 2, 1000.

5. Ibid., 994.

6. Clarke, *Story,* 217.

7. Ida Friederike Görres, *The Hidden Face: A Study of St. Thérèse of Lisieux,* trans. by Richard and Clara Winston (San Francisco: Ignatius Press, 2003), 189.

I

Story of a Soul

1. After their mother's death, Thérèse chose Pauline (now Mother Agnes) as her new "Mama."

2. Clarke, *Story,* 13.

3. Thérèse is using the numbering system that Catholic Bibles of her time typically used, which varies from others commonly used today.

4. Clarke, *Story,* 15.

5. Ibid., 16–17.

6. Clarke, *Letters,* vol. 2, 1209.

7. Ibid., 1211.

8. Clarke, *Letters,* vol. 1, 113.

9. Clarke, *Story,* 30.

II

The Tragic Loss of a Mother

1. A cousin by marriage.

2. A maid in the Martin family until Zélie Martin's death.

3. Clarke, *Story,* 33–35.

III

A Prophetic Sign

1. A title that Thérèse used for her father; in turn, he called her his Queen.

2. This vision, which occurred in the summer of 1879 or 1880, took place in broad daylight, not in a dream. M. Martin was on a business trip at Alençon.

3. A servant in the Martin residence.

4. His illness during the last five years of his life affected his mental faculties, resulting in his stay in a psychiatric hospital.

5. Clarke, *Story,* 45–48.

IV

Painful Separations

1. Clarke, *Story,* 57.

2. Ibid., 58–59.

3. Ibid., 88.

4. Clarke, *Letters,* vol. 1, 151.

5. At this point, Thérèse suffered from scruples.

6. Clarke, *Story,* 88.

7. Clarke, *Letters,* vol. 1, 254–55.

8. "She went to express her desires to the Mother Superior, who encouraged her to enter immediately . . ." (note of Mother Agnes of Jesus).

9. Clarke, *Story,* 91–92.

10. Cf. Marie Baudouin-Croix, *Léonie Martin: A Difficult Life* (Dublin: Veritas Publications, 1993), 27ff.

11. Clarke, *Letters,* vol. 1, 275–76.

V

Emotional Trials

1. Görres, *Hidden Face,* xx.

2. The cook for the Guérin family.

3. Clarke, *Story,* 60–61.

4. Ibid., 61–63.

5. Louis Martin had these Masses celebrated for Thérèse's cure.

6. Clarke, *Story,* 65–66.

7. Clarke, *Letters,* vol. 1, 171–172.

VI

Illness of an Aging Parent

1. Symbolic language referring to the day when the religious is consecrated to God through her vows.

2. Saturday, June 23, 1888, M. Martin disappeared without notifying anyone. Céline and her uncle, M. Guérin, found him at Le Havre on June 27.

3. Clarke, *Story,* 152–154.

4. Clarke, *Letters,* vol. 1, 479.

5. Céline continued to live with and care for her elderly father until his death. Only then did she enter Carmel, although she had revealed her plans to him beforehand.

6. Clarke, *Story,* 154–155.

7. Ibid., 156–157. On February 12, 1889, M. Martin had to leave Lisieux to enter a mental health institution.

8. Clarke, *Letters,* vol. 1, 530.

9. Ibid., 533–34.

10. Ibid., 534–35.

11. Ibid., 536.

12. Ibid., 537.

13. Ibid., 540.

14. Ibid., 543.

15. Clarke, *Story,* 157. The two little exiles were Léonie and Céline, who boarded at the orphanage of Saint Vincent de Paul, close to Bon Sauveur, to be near their father.

16. Clarke, *Letters,* vol. 1, 557.

17. Clarke, *Letters,* vol. 2, 875.

18. Clarke, *Story,* 177.

19. Donald Kinney, trans., *The Poetry of Saint Thérèse of Lisieux* (Washington, D.C.: ICS Publications, 1995), 61–63.

20. An affectionate nickname. The Bérésina was a river in Russia, the site of a disaster during Napoleon's retreat in 1812. Louis Martin's grandfather was in Napoleon's army.

VII

Love and Abandonment

1. Clarke, *Story,* 177–179.

VIII

The Night of Faith

1. Thérèse addressed the third section of *Story of a Soul* to Mother Marie de Gonzague, the Prioress re-elected after Mother Agnes of Jesus.

2. This refers to her temptation against faith and hope, which lasted from Easter 1896 until her death.

3. Clarke, *Story,* 210–14.

4. John Clarke, trans., *St. Thérèse of Lisieux: Her Last Conversations* (Washington, D.C.: ICS Publications, 1977), 257–58.

IX

Final Illness

1. Clarke, *Letters,* vol. 1, 94.

2. Clarke, *Conversations,* 102.

3. Ibid., 272–273.

4. Ibid., 278.

5. Clarke, *Letters,* vol. 2, 1145–46.

6. Ibid., 1142.

7. Ibid., 1186.

X

Source of Strength

1. Clarke, *Story,* 179.

2. Ibid., 200.

3. Ibid., 242.

4. Ibid., 243.

5. Kinney, *Poetry,* 90, 92.

Bibliography

Baudouin-Croix, Marie. *Léonie Martin: A Difficult Life.* Dublin: Veritas, 1993 (French edition 1989 by Les Editions du Cerf).

Bro, Bernard. *Saint Thérèse of Lisieux: Her Family, Her God, Her Message.* Translated by Anne Englund Nash. San Francisco: Ignatius Press, 2003.

Clarke, John, trans. *Letters of St. Thérèse of Lisieux, General Correspondence,* vol.1 *(1877–1890).* Washington, D.C.: ICS Publications, 1982.

―――. *Letters of St. Thérèse of Lisieux, General Correspondence,* vol. 2 *(1890–1897).* Washington, D.C.: ICS Publications, 1988.

―――. *St. Thérèse of Lisieux: Her Last Conversations.* Washington, D.C.: ICS Publications, 1977.

―――. *Story of a Soul: The Autobiography of St. Thérèse of Lisieux.* 3rd ed. Washington, D.C.: ICS Publications, 1996.

Görres, Ida Friederike. *The Hidden Face: A Study of St. Thérèse of Lisieux.* English edition translated by Richard and Clara Winston. San Francisco: Ignatius Press, 2003.

Kane, Aletheia, trans. *The Prayers of St. Thérèse of Lisieux*. Washington, D.C.: ICS Publications, 1997.

Kinney, Donald, trans. *The Poetry of Saint Thérèse of Lisieux*. Washington, D.C.: ICS Publications, 1995.

BOOKS & MEDIA

A mission of the Daughters of St. Paul

As apostles of Jesus Christ, evangelizing today's world:

We are CALLED to holiness
by God's living Word and Eucharist.

We COMMUNICATE the Gospel message
through our lives and through all
available forms of media.

We SERVE the Church
by responding to the hopes and needs
of all people with the Word of God,
in the spirit of St. Paul.

For more information visit our Web site:
www.pauline.org.

Pauline
BOOKS & MEDIA

The Daughters of St. Paul operate book and media centers at the following addresses. Visit, call, or write the one nearest you today, or find us on the World Wide Web, www.pauline.org.

CALIFORNIA

3908 Sepulveda Blvd, Culver City, CA 90230	310-397-8676
2650 Broadway Street, Redwood City, CA 94063	650-369-4230
5945 Balboa Avenue, San Diego, CA 92111	858-565-9181

FLORIDA

145 S.W. 107th Avenue, Miami, FL 33174	305-559-6715

HAWAII

1143 Bishop Street, Honolulu, HI 96813	808-521-2731
Neighbor Islands call:	866-521-2731

ILLINOIS

172 North Michigan Avenue, Chicago, IL 60601	312-346-4228

LOUISIANA

4403 Veterans Memorial Blvd, Metairie, LA 70006	504-887-7631

MASSACHUSETTS

885 Providence Hwy, Dedham, MA 02026	781-326-5385

MISSOURI

9804 Watson Road, St. Louis, MO 63126	314-965-3512

NEW YORK

64 W. 38th Street, New York, NY 10018	212-754-1110

PENNSYLVANIA

Philadelphia—relocating	215-676-9494

SOUTH CAROLINA

243 King Street, Charleston, SC 29401	843-577-0175

VIRGINIA

1025 King Street, Alexandria, VA 22314	703-549-3806

CANADA

3022 Dufferin Street, Toronto, ON M6B 3T5	416-781-9131

¡También somos su fuente para libros,
videos y música en español!